CHAOS

ALSO BY CHARITY WHAN

In Search of the Music Man

CHAOS

Charity Whan

Designed by Mark Pate
Photography by Lisa Fonville, Hemlock House, Inc.

ISBN: 979-8-218-78136-1

Printed in the United States of America

TO HOME

i turned my back on that place,

because it brought to mind

only my mistakes.

i've burned my bridges,

and now i have no way home.

i'll never be able to say it enough,

but i'm sorry to all the people i hurt

while i was hurting.

CONTENTS

INTRODUCTION

It's a set of new pages, though it starts with old wounds. How do I put this to you? How do I explain what I feel right now? A peace, simple as that.

I don't understand it either. Two months of hysteria, of gut-splitting panic, of crawling through every hour like I was being flayed from the inside out. Screams so deep they nearly killed me, but I had to keep them captive. Screams for the heartbreak. Screams for the hunger. Because, god help me, I have been so fucking hungry. And nothing has been enough.

Today, I am calm. Even as I walk straight into the fire.

If you had told me two months ago that I would cheat on my husband, you would have seen the laughter leak from my bones. This could not have been possible. Yet I did. And I did it with someone I truly shouldn't have. Someone close. Someone who will never be gone from my life. Jenna asked if I could pretend. If I could trick myself into believing it was just some stranger, some disposable body I could easily forget. I've done it before, after all.

I want that. I do. I want to jettison him, the act, the feelings right out into the atmosphere where not even the echo of them can survive. I want to say his name like it means nothing. But her brother is not nothing.

And her asking me to pretend is like asking me to dismantle myself, piece by piece, brick by brick, until there's nothing left—only the hollow shape of the woman I used to be. I can't do that. And as I sit here now, I have no idea what I'm moving toward. But perhaps the moving itself is enough to quiet the devil dancing inside me.

ICE
THE
FIRE

i burned it down,

then mourned the smoke.

i was the arsonist and the ash,

again and again.

THE PRESCRIPTION

I had long since lost my innocence, if I ever had it at all. Maybe for a time as a child, when the world was still sympathetic and simple, when hands reached out for me only to hold, not to take. But that moment passed. I learned things no child should have to before they're ready. By the time I met Tyler, I was already something else. A woman with too many lives inside her. Some feral, some soft, none of them clean.

Tyler wasn't trusting—life had made sure of that. He'd been hurt before. Not in the same ways I had, but enough to leave some cracks. He was fragile in a way that made him retreat rather than lash out. Inward, timid, always watching, never stepping forward. A loner, although I don't think he wanted to be. I think he wanted to be seen, to be understood, but he didn't know how to offer himself up to the world.

Then I saw him, I saw his innocence. And I loved him for it.

His innocence wasn't naïve, wasn't built on blind faith or ignorance. It was something different, something rare. A new hope, buried beneath years of self-protection. A gentleness that hadn't been hardened into cruelty. He wasn't untouched by pain, by any means, but he hadn't let it turn into bitterness. He still wanted to believe in things, even if he didn't always let himself.

His innocence wasn't some cheap high for me. No, it was the kind of drug they give you when you're sick. The one with the long, unpronounceable name, the one that makes the edges softer, makes the pain manageable. I was sick. I'd been sick for years. And he was everything I needed if I was ever going to find a way to heal.

I dosed myself on everything about him. The way he hesitated before speaking, like he wasn't sure his words mattered. The way he let me in, just a little, like someone cracking a window in a locked house. The way he wanted connection but didn't know how to ask for it.

He loved me the way only someone who had been hurt but still hoped could love—cautiously, gently, completely.

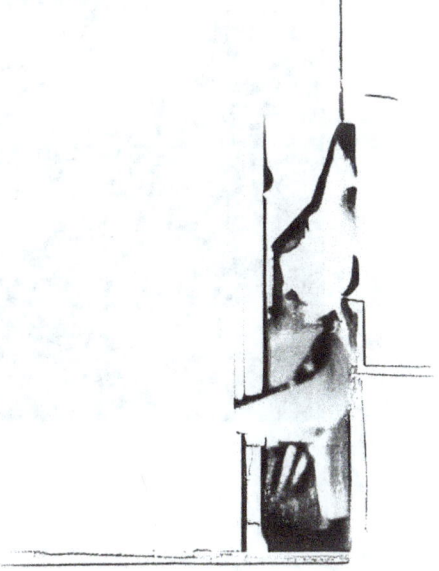

HEAVEN

when the first pains

of my transformation were gone,

i found myself healing in his home,

a small studio in trendy Hillcrest.

i couldn't do much,

so we'd lie in his bed,

(it was just his bed then)

and next to him, half-naked,

my fresh scars laid bare

beside the old wounds

he was just beginning to show,

i knew—

he was heaven.

OLALLIEBERRY JAM

you are olallieberry jam,
a sweetness born of wild things
that ripen when no one's watching.

i find you in strange places—
the market in San Luis Obispo
under the blue tent
next to the Gathering Place,
or near a wooden sign
nailed to a wine barrel
outside Half Moon Bay.

you are the crooked road,
the careful mapmaker,
the scribbled legend i follow
with trembling fingers
and a tired heart.

you are the unexpected country
i was always meant to find.

vows

i love you because the earth turns round the sun.

because the winters flow into springs,

and the air clears after a storm.

because only my love for you,

despite the gift of gravity,

keeps me from falling

off this earth into another dimension.

i love you because it's the natural way of things.

i love you like the habit i picked up as a child

of narrating my life in my head.

because i drink a glass of water every morning,

and strike my keyboard intently throughout the day.

because i take my coffee with cream.

because you keep my feet warm when life is a mess.

i love you because i don't want it any other way.

i am helpless in my love for you.

i am amazed i can resist locking you away in a room

where your voice sounds through the walls forever,

saying, "i'm here."

i love you because it's been so good for so long

that if i didn't love you,

i'd have to be born again.

i am pitiful in my love for you.

i love you because you, with all your magic,

were determined that i would love you.

because you made me want to love you,

more than i love my privacy, my freedom,

my commitments, and responsibilities.

i love you because i changed my life to love you.

i love you. i love you. i love you.

FIND ME

find me beautiful,

even now, even here,

in this house

where the doors don't close right anymore,

where the floors creak

under the burden of what we don't say.

find me beautiful when the lights flicker,

when the rooms feel too large,

when the windows shake in the wind

and my body curls into itself.

find me beautiful in the morning,

when i stand in the kitchen,

waiting for the coffee to brew,

staring

at the space on the couch you always sit.

find me beautiful in the night,

when i leave the porch light on,

even though i don't know

when you're coming home.

find me beautiful,

not just in memory,

in some photograph

of who i used to be.

find me beautiful now,

while i am here,

while the house still holds us,

while i am asking.

stay.

TYLER'S PLAYLIST

there's a woman
in a narrow house
where every room once played music.

she doesn't live there exactly,
she waits there.
barefoot, listening,
collecting songs in her pocket,
letting the notes press themselves
against her body.

some women are held by hands,
but she is held by sound.
by melodies that live in the small of her back,
verses that know her name
and hers alone.

she never asked for promises.
only the songs.
only that he keep sending them,
so she could wear them
like a second skin.

but then the house went quiet.

not all at once—

one room at a time,

like lights failing in a storm.

first the hallway.

then the kitchen.

then the small beige room

with the record player

that always skipped.

no warning.

no goodbye.

just a house full of doors

she's afraid to open

because none of them sing.

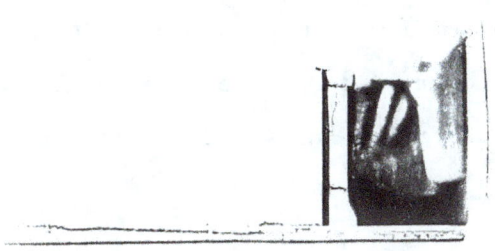

WILDFIRE

California stays the same. So does Tyler.

He's such a steady man. Predictable in the way a person becomes when you stop looking too closely. He waits for me. He texts me in the morning, telling me to be safe. He loves me with the precision of clocking in—same time, same tone, every day. I used to believe that was enough.

Hell, maybe it was.

But love gets restless when no one's listening.

I came to Illinois for a few days—a break. Illinois is my escape when my world becomes too much, when only Jenna—my friend, my found sister—can ease the ache. There, I never expect much: just a spot on the couch next to her and a few shots in a comfortable little dive where I have a standing offer to bartend. I entertain that thought, ever so slightly.

We're in that little dive now, where I always feel at home. I slip out onto the patio, inhaling the cool air as I gaze at the grain silos across the tracks. A smile creeps in. I let loose the part of me I keep hidden in California—the small-town country girl who once dreamed of a different life. I think of that life in this moment.

And when I feel a presence sit next to me on the bench, and wrap an arm around me, there is no need for me to look to see who it is. I know, every inch of my body knows, has known since the moment he walked through the door. So, I continue to stare at the silos, placing my hand on his leg.

He spoke to me of longing, and god knows it wasn't poetry, but the way it sounded. The timing. The way my body tuned itself to his voice like it had been waiting all along. Not for love. Not for meaning. Just contact. A wildfire burning out of control—I couldn't stop it.

Now I walk around pretending my skin isn't buzzing. I call my husband and tell him I miss him, and part of me truly does. But another part—

the one I can't confess—remains
back in that moment,
thinking about the way his
fingers brushed my face like he
had every right to.

Tyler waits for me at home, but
I'm out here staring at the trees,
waiting to see how fast they'll
burn.

this is what it feels like

to step out of one wreck

into the memory of another.

THE LONG HUG

now we are nothing

but arms and breath,

in silence thick enough to keep

whatever this was

from breaking into sound.

this is what it feels like

to step out of one wreck

into the memory of another.

a pause becomes a question.

a question becomes a wound.

no answers

or names for this.

only the shadow of a feeling

that might have mattered

if it hadn't arrived so late.

A LITTLE WHILE LONGER...

i called him *home*
the moment we met,
when he worshipped me reverently,
when his silence made room for me.
and i kept calling him *home*
long after i started sleeping
beside him like a stranger
afraid to ask for warmth.

what do we do
when peace and chaos dwell together?
when they share the same table,
peace on one side,
chaos on the other,
you in the middle,
just trying to sustain?

why do i stay?
because he is the mirror
where i last saw myself whole.
i want to know
that version of me

a little longer,

the one who made sense

in his eyes,

the one who called him *home*

and believed it.

PARADISE

The air in Cancun feels like a punishment, dense with heat and moisture, clinging to my skin like guilt. Even the waves, crashing in their predictable rhythm, mock the bedlam inside me.

I let Tyler take my hand as we walk along the shore, his grip warm but absent, the touch of someone who assumes love lasts forever. He talks, but his words scatter about in my mind. I nod and smile, hiding behind the mask I've worn for a couple of years. Beneath it, my body betrays me—burning and restless.

Under this glaring Mexican sun, everything is too bright, and too clear. Tyler wears his happiness effortlessly, oblivious to the storm I've carried with me across the miles. When he kisses me, I can't feel it. When he pulls me toward our hotel bed, I fake exhaustion from the heat, from travel, from the food and alcohol I keep gorging myself on. I've grown skilled at excuses. He's grown used to believing them.

Tonight, I let him touch me. He starts with familiar gestures—his mouth grazing my shoulder, his hand trailing over my hip. I close my eyes and try to meet him halfway, but it's as though my body is a locked door, the key lost in another man's pocket. I picture that other man—the sharpness of his jawline, the weight of his body against mine, the way he looked at me like I was alive.

I am gone. I am in another room, another city, another life. I am breathless again, but not from this. When I shudder, it is not for Tyler, though I let him think it is. He falls asleep with his arm draped over my waist, his love heavy and suffocating.

Tomorrow, we'll drink strawberry margaritas by the pool and take photos we'll never look at again. I'll wear my swimsuit like a baptismal robe, letting the water lap over me while I pretend it can wash me clean.

HOUSE OF METAMORPHOSIS

there are clouds
over the House of Metamorphosis.
i take that personally,
as with most things.

because i am a shapeshifter.
and while that detail
is a different story entirely,
here is what you need to know.
i am a survivalist.
i am a woman with a thousand forms
and none of them seem
my own.

but the Universe
has a sense of humor.
it keeps showing me
a form i will never take—
mother.

the memory comes to me

in the checkout line.

in the yogurt aisle.

on Thursdays.

at the little booth in the vintage market

that sells the dolls.

i am a shapeshifter.

and none of my forms

were made to hold

something

that cannot shift with me.

WANT

you know what the worst feeling is?

i can't get right with it.

i can't sit, i can't breathe.

i can't stop thinking.

i can't stop *wanting*.

wanting to see him again,

wanting him to tell me,

"i've wanted to do that all day" again.

to believe he's thought of me

just once

so i'm not this pathetic, feral thing

digging at the hours,

gnawing on every second

since *August*

when everything went sideways

and i needed him so bad

i nearly broke open.

i'm combusting.

my blood's inventing new places to pulse,

my skin can't hold me in,

my jaw aches from clenching,

my goddamn *eyes* burn

every time i blink.

i want, i want, i *want*!

i have no idea what to do

with all this fucking want.

DEEP BRUISE

i have this bruise that reminds me of you.

deep and painful, hot under the skin.

the damn thing won't heal.

a month's gone by and it remains,

stubborn and unforgiving,

like the way you exist in the world.

but i have to admit,

there's a part of me

that loves this sort of thing.

give me any pain

singing in colors of flesh

if it reminds me

i'm still living.

WHAT I WOULDN'T DO

there is no world in which this works.

but i'd still throw myself in

like it wouldn't break me to land wrong.

i'd drag a sky over our heads,

patch it together with everything we've wanted

and never had.

i'd shape the ground with my bare hands,

call it devotion,

call it madness.

every mountain would rise

from the ruins of what we've burned.

every river would churn

from the hell we've survived before this.

your love wouldn't make me a fool.

it would make me a world-builder.

BEYOND THE MOON

the full moon hangs tonight.
i see it and think of you,
how distance is now measured in ache,
not miles.

every day,
i feel the impatience of my wings.
they twitch against my back,
like something riotous,
trying to break free.
what good is a body
that craves what it can't have?

the moon knows
it will wane and wax again.
even the sky knows how to let go.
but i am all hands and heart,
grasping for a man who hasn't come.

maybe i will never reach the place
beyond the moon where you exist.
still, i look up from the street,
knowing it's all that i can do.

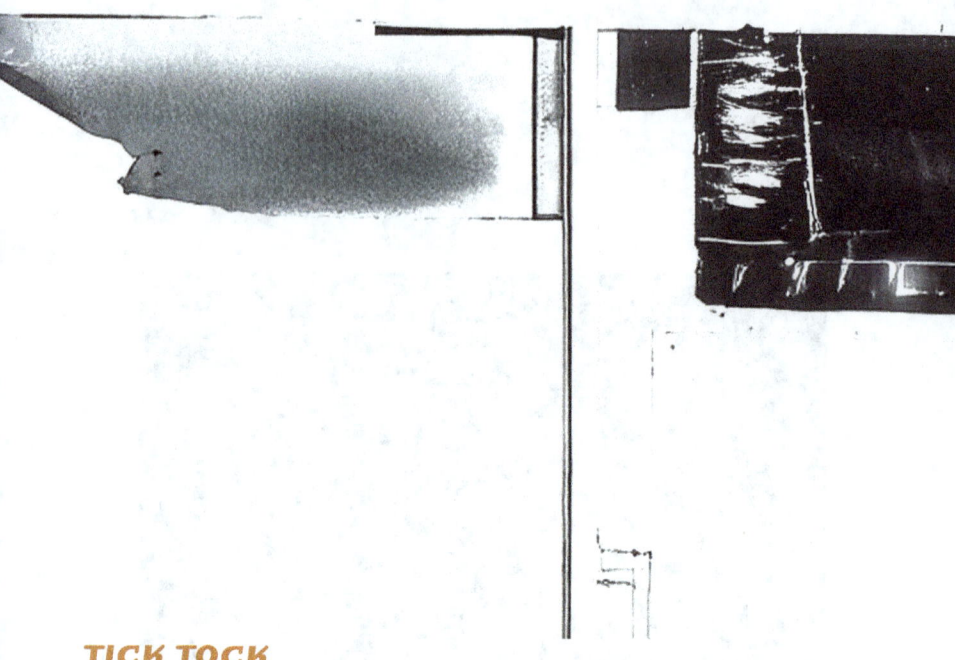

TICK TOCK

Tick tock, tick tock. The clock on my laptop flips from 2:04 to 2:05. It's digital, but I hear the sound anyway—time mocking me. Another minute passes and I can't bring myself to do it. What would I even say? That I wanted something and took it, knowing it would cost me everything? The words don't form. They just *hover*. Like smoke.

I take a long drag from my vape and exhale a slow cloud of vapor. I watch it drift, twist my fingers through it like I'm stirring my thoughts— trying to grab hold of one, but they keep slipping. Or maybe I don't want to hold onto any of them. Maybe this little ritual keeps me from having to look too closely.

Tyler. Him. The sex. The silence. The goddamn weight of it all. Even now, I can't tell what it was. A mistake? A beginning? Or just one of those moments that refuses to sit long enough to become.

The image of telling Tyler—of saying it out loud—crashes through all the mundane things: the laundry waiting at home, the unread emails piling up, the incomplete projects that suddenly feel like a shield. I bury myself in the ordinary so I don't have to explode my whole life.

I think I want to rip this part of me open and see what survives. I'm terrified of what happens after. Of the mess. Of the other kind of banishment that comes once everything is out in the open and no one knows what to say.

God help me, let that be the thing that makes me new. Let that be the thing that transforms me forever.

THE QUIET WAR

it's not the shouting that gets you,

not the slammed doors

or the broken dishes.

those are easy,

loud enough to give names.

it's the silence,

silence that sinks its teeth in,

silence that leaves you guessing

if you're the one bleeding

or imagining the wound.

it's a slow war,

a room where the walls lean in too close,

a stare across the dining table

that says nothing

and everything.

and the worst silence,

the one that rips you,

is the silence in your own chest,

so deep you forget who you're fighting.

him, yourself,

the spirit of absence

that never learned how to leave.

some nights,

it's so quiet you can hear

the sound of your own solitude.

a whisper with no breath.

a war with no victor.

WINTER MEMORIES

Southern California has its own version of winter, but it's not the same as home. It doesn't bite or embrace. It brushes past, indifferent. Winter in the Midwest lingers, like a familiar face in a crowd, waiting for you to notice it. It's a season you wear, not just endure.

I think about the place I call home, and how it beckons me in a voice I can't ignore. The way the streets seem quieter under the weight of snow or the heavy press of gray skies. The kind of quiet that leaves space for reflection. Sometimes too much.

Jenna is there, grounding the place like an anchor. I picture her laughing in her kitchen, pouring a vodka soda, the warmth of her house spreading through the phone when we talk. She makes it feel like home is still mine, even though I've been away for so long.

And then there's him. He's always there in the memories, tangled up in that place, the two now inseparable. We've known each other twenty years, long enough that his presence has blurred into the fabric of that home I miss so much. When I think about him, I wonder if I miss him for who he is, or just the idea of him. Do I love him, or is it the idea of loving someone who belongs to that place, someone who makes it feel more like mine again?

I can see the way he moves through winter. The way his breath hangs in the air in clouds, the way his charming laugh cuts through the cold. I can't tell if these memories are mine or ones I've pieced together from longing.

California is golden and wide, but it doesn't always feel like home. Not in the way the Midwest burrows into your bones. Winter at home feels closer to real love—harsh but beautiful, imperfect but honest. Southern California is like a daydream—soft, fleeting, insubstantial.

Tonight, the air outside cools just enough to remind me of what I'm missing. I open the door to feel the chill on my body, but it's not the same. I close my eyes and think of home. I don't know if I'm imagining him standing there or if he's standing in the shadow of a memory I haven't let go of yet.

REFLECTIONS

there's a crack

in the mirror behind the bar,

the kind that splits your reflection

into too many versions of yourself.

the blurry one

who orders another shot,

the loud one

spilling stories you swore you'd forget,

the hesitant one

watching from the corner,

like you don't belong to yourself.

the speakers spill over

with a sound half-broken,

but they moan out truth.

you are both

the sinner and the saint.

there's a woman outside the bar,

smoking as if she's waiting

for the past to clear.

you can see it in her eyes.

she's waiting for nothing,

and you understand.

you can be both

the fight

and the apology.

the one who left

and the one who stayed.

the wound

and the whiskey poured into it.

ICE THE FIRE, BURY THE SEA

i sat peaceful in a quiet love for a time.

until flirty Chaos wrapped his arms around me

and asked me if i wanted to be free.

but freedom is never free,

and Chaos never really leaves.

because when his form is gone,

his silence remains.

and i realize that answers

can be found in that hollow gift,

truth hidden in the spaces

between words left unsaid.

so now, i sit here alone,

heaving with grief.

his thunderous quiet to ice the fire,

my silent screams to bury the sea.

I wonder
what kind of woman
I am, that I keep
believing love can
be salvaged

if I put my body on a plane and land it in
the right place. That I think proximity
can fix what distance exposed.

TIME TO THINK

I don't know how to explain the kind of desperation that makes a woman buy a plane ticket just to feel a man look at her. But I've done it. More than once.

The second time I went back to Illinois wasn't because I was sure he would welcome me with open arms—deep down, I knew better. I went back because I needed to know. It felt impossible to move on while this door was still cracked open. I needed to feel it slam shut.

The thing is, I have a history of this. Of chasing ghosts in cities that don't want me. I've gotten on planes with my heart in my throat, thinking if I showed up, things would make sense. It has never worked.

There was a man in D.C. once—always too busy—but when he told me to come, I went. We ate hot chicken wings, drank beer that stung going down, and sang new gospel in his kitchen. It felt like something sacred in the moment. And in the morning, he smiled from across the bed, and said, "It's time to go home."

And before I married my first husband, I flew west to see another man. We saw Jerry Springer on Rodeo Drive, and I told him I loved him. I told him to choose me, because I would choose him in every lifetime. He beamed, and in the morning, staring at me from across my hotel bed, he said, "It's time to go home."

That sentence has followed me like a curse. I show up full of feeling, and they press the end into my palm like that's what I asked for. Nevertheless, I keep doing it. I tell myself I'm just looking for answers. But I just want to be chosen back. I want someone to be so sure of me that they don't let me walk out the door. That they say, *stay.*

I think about that every time I'm at the gate, boarding pass in hand, trying to look normal when I feel anything but. I wonder what kind of woman I am, that I keep believing love can be salvaged if I put my body on a plane and land it in the right place. That I think proximity can fix what distance exposed.

But I go because I don't know what else to do with the pain. I go because the hushfall drives me mad, and airports feel like motion, like I'm at least doing *something*. Even if it always ends the same.

This time on the way home, I didn't cry. I just sat there, staring ahead, knowing that the long journey home would give me time to think.

DEVOTION

i'd been listening.
i'd been waiting for some sign
i was right all along.

that it wasn't madness,
wasn't loneliness in a fleeting shape,
wasn't just me
clawing through aloofness
and calling it restraint.

all i heard
was my own voice
on a loop in the void,
saying:
he will choose you.
he has to.
why else would you be here,
hemorrhaging like this?

i believed it
because the truth
was too brutal,

that i built a temple

from scraps

and begged him

to be its god.

what i should have heard

is the only truth

that has ever stayed true.

no one is coming to save you.

and i will rest in the remains

of my devotion,

naked in a room

that won't stop echoing

with all the things

i made myself believe.

THE RESCUE

i rehearsed the rescue
until i couldn't tell the difference
between hope and hallucination.

funny how easy it is
to mistake your own voice
for someone else's love,
how the things we say to survive
can become the very things
that murder us in our beds.

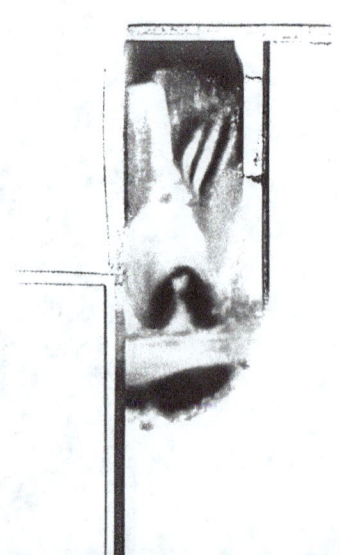

LITTLE WHITE GIRL

i can't explain my desire,
why it calls to me now.

i am a beast—
desirous,
egotistical,
maniacal,
unyielding.
completely driven by need.
libidinal hunger—
a seed planted as a child
that what my body feels
is the only thing that's real.

i have no mind.

only flesh,
and hours to kill,
hating myself.

All we could do was sit at that table and scream, avoiding our reflections—licking what was left off the mirror, realizing this wasn't love, it was need.

WATCH THE WORLD BURN

I realize only now, it was never going to work when all we both wanted to do was watch the world burn. It was never going to be right, or good, or decent when we didn't feel right, or good, or decent.

And I see that the reason it all even happened in the first place was because on the day that changed everything, I felt a kind of peace. I felt comfortable in a place my heart has always lived. And he felt at home in that peace.

There was no peace this time, and there was never going to be again. And all we could seem to do was try to make the other see that our pain was somehow bigger and more important than the other's. All we could do was sit at that table and scream, avoiding our reflections—licking what was left off the mirror, realizing this wasn't love, it was need.

You can only find hate in a place like that. But I know I don't want to hate him, and I don't want to hate Tyler. And most importantly, I don't want to hate myself.

I think, in some way, that is exactly what I went back there to do. I went to do something that would make me loathe myself. Because being with him that day didn't. I don't regret our time together. And I know that the tears I've shed have not been for the pain I will cause, but rather for the pain of knowing that happiness still exists out there somewhere. I just haven't found a way to keep it.

I KNOW

i know what it's like to feel like you can't go on,
that life just isn't worth it anymore.

but this is not that.

it's not that i don't want to live anymore.
it's that i don't want to keep living like this.

A FRESH HELL

When we are wrapped up in our own frantic thoughts, the physical world around us can feel like a dream…there, but not there—alive, but distant—buzzing with sound, but sound that almost seems to flow from a place you'll never know.

I've had too many hours, too many days in the last few months where I've lost all sense of myself. Perhaps that's why I haven't spent much time outside of our little condo in Normal Heights. Somewhere, subconsciously, I know that if I go out there and live this version of my life in the world, they will see that I'm a fraud. They will see the lie, and how it has made me decay.

What fresh hell is this? It feels like dying.

If I'm lucky, I'll only regret the choices that I've made. Until then, I suppose I will die a little every day.

SOMEWHERE BETWEEN

it was easy,

one minute you're going to the gym,

taking the dog out,

checking the mail like it matters,

and the next,

you're pacing the length of your room,

talking to no one

or god

or whatever listens

when you are unshod and unraveling.

there was a week or three months

where i forgot how to sleep.

where i sat on the edge of my bed,

knowing if i lay down,

i would dream myself inside out.

i moved like a specter

and knew better than to say so.

but i wasn't haunting.

i was being haunted.

by time, by consequence,

by the way my body had turned against me,

leaving me bleeding, *empty*.

it is easy, you see,

to wake up sane,

to put on your coat,

to remember to lock the door,

then find yourself in a world

where your own hands

don't belong to you anymore,

where your own body

doesn't answer to its name,

where you stop asking,

what happens next?

because you're too afraid

to know the answer.

I DIDN'T LIE

I was already crying when I asked Tyler to sit down. The kind of crying that feels like your body is slowly letting go of what it can't hold anymore. I was on the bed, twisted up in myself, wet face turned to the wall, "Ty, we need to have a hard conversation."

He didn't ask what about. He didn't have to.

That's the thing no one talks about. How the hardest part isn't saying the words. It's sitting in the certainty that comes before them, knowing they're already true. He looked at me—not scared, not angry—only knowing. We both felt what was coming. We just had to get through it.

I told him. Time paused and the air thickened. My body felt like it was made of glass. I'd spent months building the courage to shatter the version of myself he thought he knew. Its breaking spoke a language I didn't understand.

Eventually it dawned on me—the cage had never been made of marriage. It was made of thoughts. Of decisions not made. Of truths not spoken. And sometimes, the truth is the harder you hold onto somebody, the lonelier you feel.

I had been buried under the weight of a choice I hadn't made yet. The pressure of pretending everything was fine, of smiling through a life that didn't fit anymore. And it's amazing how fast a single choice can go from feeling like a goddamn death sentence, to releasing you from bonds you didn't even know you had.

There was pain. There had to be. But I'll do my best to remember the first day, not the last. The first time we kissed under the lights in Long Beach. The way he used to trace circles on the back of my thigh when he wanted attention. The way he sent me songs to tell me that he loved me.

He loved me gently. I broke his heart softly. But ultimately, I didn't lie. I didn't hide. And I think, in the end, that mattered.

WISDOM

at some point in our lives

we all make the drastic assumption

that because there is something in us to hate,

there is nothing in us to love.

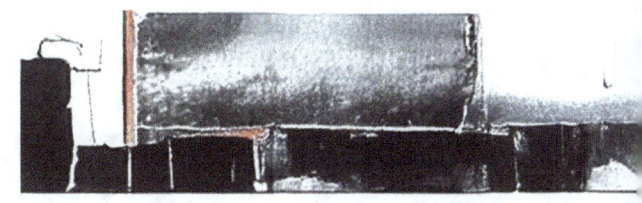

BURY
THE
SEA

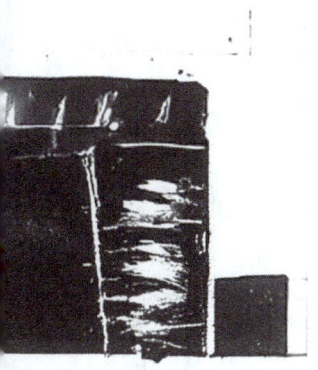

there's a grief that follows clarity.

a salt that settles after the squall.

yet we wade back in,

not to drown,

but to remember who we are.

THE END OF THE WORLD

some people bounce back.
they get knocked down,
brush it off
like they saw the hit coming.

not *me*.

i fall like the whole planet
went sideways.
a silence feels like exile.
a criticism feels like death.
a call that never comes
is a fucking funeral.

my body doesn't care
what my mind knows.
it still folds—
tight, ashamed—
every time i have to come home
to myself.

two divorces later
and i still haven't figured out
how to build a spine
out of all that rot.

and the worst part is,
i know i'll do it again.
next week.
tomorrow.
later tonight.

it's not the end of the world.
i just wish it didn't feel like it
every goddamn time.

WAIT IN THE FIRE

i never leave the burning.
it's warmer than stillness,
at least here
i can feel something.

ash collects in my collarbones.
i call it memory.
call it love
when it's really just
staying put
in a place that never asks me to.

no one calls me out of it.
no arms stretch through the smoke.
i keep waiting.
for rescue, i suppose
or maybe just for proof
that someone sees.

it's not even about return anymore.
it's ritual.
the way some pray,

or drink,

or trace the outline

of an old scar

to remember how it felt

before it healed wrong.

still, i stay.

still, i burn.

and every time i think of walking away,

i wonder the woman i would be

if i stopped waiting in the fire.

ALONE

i've come home
to find pieces of who i *used to be*
gone.

i move through the house
like it still belongs to both of us,
but the silence has chosen sides.

strange how suddenly *our* becomes *my*,
and the thing that made me so hopeful for a time
now creeps into the space called *alone*.

CHARITY ISN'T HOME

Charity isn't home right now. She's somewhere between aisle seven and the ninth circle of hell, muttering to herself about lactose-free milk and trying not to scream into the refrigerator door.

She's got her sunglasses on indoors, which would be fine if she didn't also have a shopping cart full of nothing but throat lozenges, carrot cake, and Tito's. Someone she sort of knows passes her and says hello. She smiles too hard, says she's "good," like it's a spell that will keep her from shattering right there between the crackers and the tortilla chips. She keeps moving. She doesn't need anything. That's the worst part. She just didn't want to sit at home by herself anymore.

She told someone recently that she's "taking time for herself." What that means is driving around listening to songs that remind her of people who no longer speak to her and pretending it's healing. It's not. But the acoustics in her Prius are excellent for screaming.

Charity used to be someone. She's not sure who, but she remembers liking her. Now she is mostly carbon and caffeine, rehashing the same three stories to whoever's unlucky enough to spend time with her. She's tired of her own voice. Tired of saying the same things and meaning none of them.

She flirts with bartenders. Not for the thrill of it—no, she wants something. She wants to know that she's wanted. That her body isn't just this vessel for guilt and decisions she can't undo. She lets their eyes linger. She lets their hands touch hers. She leans in too far and laughs too loudly, because being desired—even momentarily—is the only time she doesn't feel empty.

She hasn't cried in a while. Not because she's fine, but because the tears got bored and left. Now it's just this dull pain squatting in her ribs. Instead of therapy, she watches videos of strangers talking about healing and boundaries and growth. She saves them like she'll come back to them. She never does. But for a second, it feels like trying.

At night she lies awake, staring at the ceiling fan and wondering if anyone's ever truly known her. If she's ever really been seen. If love was something she imagined, or something she ruined.

LIKE A CORPSE

the shower beats down hard.
a death drum.
i curl into the porcelain,
skin flushed like meat,
heartbeat slow and dull.

my legs have gone numb.
the water climbs my back
like it's trying to baptize me
or drown me,
i can't tell which.
either would be a kindness.

pain doesn't scream anymore.
it waits.
pulses in the spout,
hangs in the steam,
slips into the cracks of the tile.

i keep thinking someone

will pull back the curtain.

find me like this

days later,

eyes open,

steam slowly rising off my bones.

THE DOLLHOUSE

i spent so long disappearing,
shrinking into the walls,
learning how to make loneliness
look like loyalty.

no one realizes,
i was dying a slow and excruciating death.

so, when i grasped at a different truth,
when my fingers curled around a moment
that reminded me i was still alive,
the story became simple to everyone but me.

they would have me stay,
mute and starving,
like Anna before the train,
who loved too fiercely,
who would rather throw herself
onto the steel tracks of judgment
than be caged in a life that wasn't her own.

they would have me stay,

like Nora before the door swung open,

before she realized the walls of her home

were just another kind of prison,

before she stepped into the night,

knowing the world would brand her selfish

for wanting more than a gilded cage.

i know what they'd say,

what they'd think

if they ever knew about the ending.

the part that made it easy

to turn me into something small and shameful.

let them talk.

let them reduce me

to a whisper behind the hand.

and let them know,

i would rather live the whore,

than die a bride.

THE SLOW RETURN TO MYSELF

Reawakening is not easily acquired. It is not gentle, nor seamless. It does not happen in an instant, but rather in a slow, aching timeline of undoing.

It seems it took me a lifetime to notice myself fading. It happened quietly, over years, like a shoreline eroded by waves too subtle to mark. I was there, moving through my days, fulfilling the roles expected of me. But something essential was slipping away—my femininity, my creativity, my sense of self. I didn't realize how much of me had disappeared until someone else made me feel a spark of me again.

It was touch, and breath, and joy. It was everything that reminds you of what's gone, all the things that wake up a part of you and scream that you are everything wonderful in this world. In that moment, I was seen in a way I was not being seen—not just as someone's partner, not as an obligation, but as a woman capable of stirring and being stirred. And suddenly, I couldn't unsee the truth: I had been living small. I had let myself shrink into the background of my own life.

Desire is not simple. It doesn't care for the rules you have built around yourself. It only knows what is real, what is needed, what has been neglected for too long. I had a choice—to ignore it, to push it aside, to pretend it hadn't cracked something open inside me. Or to listen.

Listening meant facing truths I wasn't ready for. It meant grief, guilt, and the undeniable weight of change. But it also meant returning to myself. The woman I had been, the one I let slip away. She was there. She had simply been waiting for me to notice her absence.

Reawakening is not easily acquired. It always demands more than we think we can give. But I see now that losing myself forever would have been harder.

I chose to return to myself.

THE NOISE I CRAVE

i was built in survival,
not born into it.
forged by women
who didn't have time to teach me
what to want,
only what to endure.

i learned love the way you learn fire,
burned fingertips, blistered instinct,
calling the singe on my skin
something holy.

the first man i ever desired
looked like the warning
on a pack of cigarettes.
and i lit him up,
over and over.
even when the smoke filled my lungs
and i couldn't breathe.
especially then.

you start to crave that kind of pain.

the kind that begs you to stay,

then dares you to survive it.

and i did.

too many times.

until i began to think

survival was the love.

then peace arrived,

not so much in a person,

but in the absence of urgency.

the pause between heartbeats

where no one needed saving,

and nothing was aflame.

i didn't know what to do with that.

i didn't trust it.

because the blaze had always

screamed louder than the truth,

i tore gentle things apart

just to hear the noise again.

no one told me

healing would feel like loss,

that the hurt wouldn't just be

for the lessons i called lovers,

but for the versions of me

who kept calling them home.

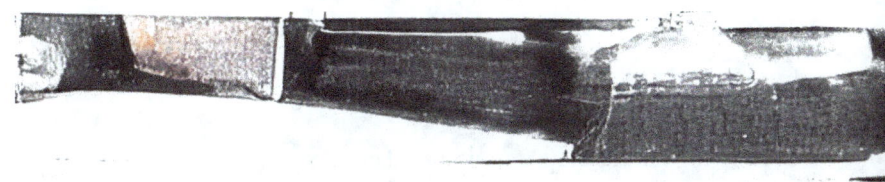

JAGGED MOLDS

try to comprehend,

for a moment,

the sheer breadth of things

we fleshy reeds can be addicted to.

i recall how my lungs would heave

with burnt air and tar

as soon as i walked into my mother's house.

my father's first beer of the morning.

the way my aunt's hand glided across

the gleaming reels of a slot machine,

a ritual only she understood.

the addiction i see most vividly,

the craving that feels like mud in my shoes

every time i try to run from its memory,

is chaos.

there are those on this earth

who can't live, breathe, or function without it.

why?

it's all they've ever known.

they were poured into a jagged mold

and formed into a piece of art

no one in their right mind would call art.

but i see them.

i see them for the wild beauty they are.

and i know i can caress them,

pull them tight to my body,

their pointed edges fitting snugly

inside the holes life has left in me.

i always think i can save them.

i always think

they will save me.

there's a tightness in the mouth,

a sharpness in the brow.

small betrayals of blood.

we call it inheritance,

it's more like residue.

smudges on bones that remind us

of all we fear.

INHERITANCE

what are we

when we look in the mirror?

ourselves?

or the shape

of all the people who left us?

some days

i pass a mirror

and stop breathing.

not because i see a person,

but because i don't.

i see something

too solid

to be a memory

and too unfamiliar

to be me.

there's a tightness in the mouth,

a sharpness in the brow.

small betrayals of blood.

we call it inheritance,

it's more like residue.

smudges on bones that remind us
of all we fear.

it's not the fear of being lost.
it's the fear of being *found*,
in people i swore
i'd never become.
but for some us,
we are what we survive.
and most survival
looks like mimicry.

i don't always know
if i'm kind.
or if i'm just tired
of being broken.
and i want,
god, i want
to be more than
an echo in the mirror.

i want to believe i'm different.

that my softness is mine.

that the ache in my chest

isn't just a hand-me-down.

but most days

i stare at the glass,

and all i see is a history

repeating itself

with better posture.

and i'm tired of carrying people

who never carried me.

MY NEW ADDRESS

i've been grateful.

i've been soft.

i've whispered "thank you"

through gritted teeth in the dark.

i've done the work.

the shadow journaling.

the moon water.

the prayers that felt like begging

in a language no one speaks anymore.

and still...

you leave my due just far enough

to make me crawl for it.

you think i haven't noticed the pattern?

the slow reveal, the quick cut.

the man who says *maybe,*

the job that says *almost,*

the trial that says *not quite yet.*

fuck you.

seriously.

i've built temples out of my own shame.

i've slept in the belly of disaster

and woken up pretending i liked the taste of it.

i don't want your cosmic breadcrumbs.

i want a goddamn meal.

i want something to stay

when i finally reach for it.

you want me to live in the chaos?

fine.

here's my new address:

right in the eye of the storm,

with the door torn off

and a name you keep forgetting.

come visit me, Universe.

come explain yourself.

DELIGHT IN DESTRUCTION

there's a moment,

right before the whole thing comes down,

where you see it.

the cracks in the foundation,

the slow bow of the beams,

the way it was never as strong

as you told yourself it was.

and that's when you decide—

not to run away from it,

not to patch it up,

but take delight in its destruction.

tear the damn thing down,

rip it apart with your own two hands,

cackle as the dust settles in your hair.

this was never meant to last,

none of it.

people mourn what they lose,

but forget to celebrate

what they get to rebuild.

so light the fucking match,

smash the goddamn glass,

say goodbye to what you've outgrown.

step forward,

barefoot and bloody in the wreckage,

ready to build again.

THE WOMEN

they've been surviving so long

it looks like grace,

but it's not grace.

it's grit, the steely kind,

the kind you don't notice

until you've already leaned on it too hard.

women.

they don't break the way men expect,

they bend, they bear it,

they carry the weight of men who call it love

when it's just need,

another hunger that never fed them back.

yet, they stay,

not because they're weak,

but because they've learned

how to hold the whole mess in their hands

without spilling a drop.

the men.

they think they're the storms,

loud and reckless,

but it's the women who know

what it means to last.

they endure men

who mistake softness for weakness,

who want them easy, pretty,

as if a wild thing could be kept.

and when they finally go,

because they always go,

they don't slam the door,

they walk away so effortlessly

you'll think they were never there.

RIVERS OF REGRET

the rivers are flowing,
twisting like veins beneath my skin,
carrying stories i cannot forget.

i bare my scars,
long and winding tributaries,
etched in moments of weakness.
poor decisions spilling like rainwater
onto a land that already knew flood.

how many bridges have crumbled?
how many banks have collapsed
under the weight of my own choices?

the rivers keep flowing, heartless,
but i remain.
a woman standing at the edge of herself,
ankles deep in Missouri mud,
watching the current carry away
all the things i cannot take back.

and yet, the water moves,
a whisper of hope—
perhaps even the most broken river
can find its way home to the sea.

ON THE TRAIN TO RENO

they used to take trains to Reno
in satin nightgowns and fox stoles,
sipping gin out of crystal
while their husbands kept the house.

that was the story.
that was the sell.

i've done it twice now
and there's no train.
just me in a borrowed apartment
with a half-dead succulent
and too many credit card receipts.

the only thing i'm sipping
is cheap wine
from a chipped glass
with a faded "happy wife"
in flaking glitter on the front.
that's the real ceremony.

sure, you can say i'm lucky.

so many love stories.

lie to me sweet.

but the truth is

they all left me weaker,

more unsure of my reflection.

always wondering

how goddamn unfair it is

to be so easy to leave.

NO MYTHS FOR WOMEN LIKE ME

what you don't know,

is the fruit was never meant for you.

even when they told you to *keep reaching*.

that was the curse.

not the hunger itself,

but the belief that one day

it would be fed.

Tantalus stood ankle-deep in the water,

throat raw from trying.

it was justice,

and he earned his ache.

i've stood there too,

barefoot in a pool of maybe,

neck craned toward something

that would always rise

just beyond my touch.

they don't make myths for women like me.

only warnings.

only quiet punishments

dressed as character arcs.

they tell you to be patient.

if you wait long enough,

the thing you lost will come back clean.

but time doesn't give.

it empties.

it thins you out

until you forget what it was

you were even starving for.

closure is a myth

we invented to keep going.

a bedtime story we read to our grief

so it doesn't tear through the walls at night.

i have loved people

who've carved their names on my flesh

and never looked back.

i begged the sky for them.

i shaped my body

into something just for them.

and i *reached* for them.

the fruit always rose.

the water fled.

and i learned the hardest truth of all—

not everything we ache for

was ever ours to hold.

INVENTORY

click.

heart.

finger.

face.

order received.

no shipping info.

no tracking number.

he writes

"you up?"

and it's enough

to make me go postal.

meanwhile,

the feed updates.

the body forgets.

the app crashes

and i delete.

reload.

i list myself again—

witty.

low maintenance.

soft.

SOLD.

the economy of misery

turns and burns.

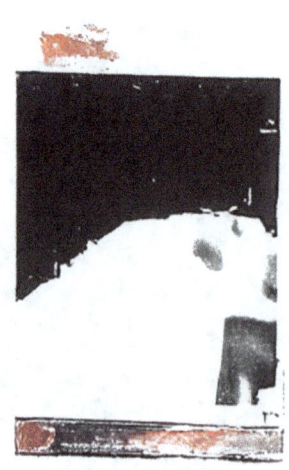

TO THE MAN WHO STOLE MY
BUKOWSKI COLLECTION

you didn't steal it.
not really.
i surrendered it like everything else.
spine-cracked, underlined, dog-eared to hell,
like i was.

you liked the one about the fighter.
said he wrote women like bruises he kept pressing.
i think i laughed.
i think i agreed.

but let's be honest,
we were never quoting poetry in bed.
it was punishment.
me, crawling back to the knife.
because the shame only stopped screaming
when your teeth were on my shoulder
and your hands were around my neck.

you weren't cruel.

that was the worst part.

cruelty, at least,

gives you something to fight.

you just…took.

and i let you.

every time.

as if somewhere in the bruising

i might earn forgiveness.

not from you.

from me.

my apartment.

white sheets and a blue duvet.

Bukowski on the nightstand

beside a half-drunk bottle of wine.

that was my church.

i knelt for communion

with no priest, no redemption.

only pain and sweat.

when you finally disappeared,

you took the books.

that was fair.

a final tithe.

let him go, i thought.

let him carry the words i once used

to justify the madness.

i'm not angry.

this isn't that kind of letter.

it's just…

there's a hole where *Love is a Dog from Hell* used to be.

and i miss it every time i catch the line

tattooed on my skin,

and remember

you never asked me what it meant.

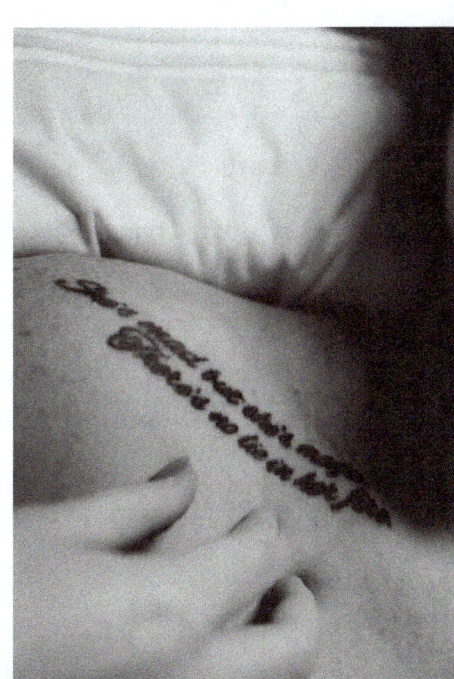

so no, you weren't a bad man.

but you were the man i let fuck me

like i owed the world an apology.

and i did.

HEALING BS

they keep saying it's a journey
like there's a damn map,
like if you keep walking long enough
you'll find the exit wound closed,
stitched up clean
by time and intention.

i told a friend
i'd been feeling like shit again,
grief pulling up a chair to brunch
like it never even left.
she looked at me, tired-eyed, and said,
"maybe we don't really heal.
maybe we just learn how to walk
without screaming."

i haven't stopped thinking about that.

sometimes
healing isn't scented candles, long baths,
online therapy.
sometimes

it's simply trying not to flinch

when someone laughs

the way he did.

it's sleeping through the night

once in a while,

calling that a win.

you know that Japanese thing,

kintsugi?

they break a bowl,

then fill the cracks with gold.

people call it beautiful.

nobody ever says

the damn thing leaks.

you don't drink from it anymore.

you put it on a shelf,

call it art,

and try not to miss what it was

before it shattered.

SEVEN MONTHS LATER

After Tyler moved out, I felt like I was collapsing, and also, strangely, like I was breathing for the first time in years.

In the beginning, this sense of relief didn't look like freedom. It looked like failure. I felt like I had taken a bat to my own life and was standing in the rubble, trying to figure out if anything was worth salvaging.

But here I am, seven months later, and the weird thing is—we're okay. Not "okay" in the way that couples patch things up and pretend it never happened. We aren't together. That part of our journey together has come to end. But we're okay in a way I didn't think was possible back then.

We talk occasionally. We check in, we laugh about old inside jokes. We still care about each other, only differently. There's no performance anymore. No pretending we're fine when we're not. No keeping score.

I think, deep down, Tyler felt trapped, too. Not by me, not entirely. But by the life we'd built that neither of us really fit inside anymore. We were good at routines. We had our traditions and we were loyal. We were safe and there was a lot of good to what we had. It was just somewhere along the way, safe started to feel stagnant. I was afraid to say it out loud because I didn't want to be the one who ruined it. And maybe that's what I did anyway. Or maybe I finally acted on feelings we were both just too polite to admit.

You know, I used to think the worst thing that could happen in a relationship was hurting the person you love. But staying when you're not fully alive? That's its own kind of violence. It's a slow bleed. A lonely path.

I don't regret telling the truth. I regret that it took me so long to be honest—with him and with myself. But even that has softened now. The guilt doesn't suffocate me anymore. The sadness doesn't demand to be fed every day. I just carry it, like a scar that no longer stings, yet knows how it got there.

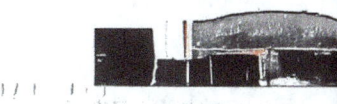

WHATEVER COMES

i've stopped checking the door.
stopped pacing the hours
like something's supposed to arrive.
there's nothing to expect but me,
and i'm already here.

i've sat in both the fire and the calm
long enough to know
neither will kill me.
i've stood at the edge
of all my endings,
and never once disappeared.

i don't need a sign.
i don't need a savior.
i don't need the promise
of a life
someone else builds.

i need only this—
the sound of my own breath,
steady and unremarkable.
evidence that whatever comes,
i will remain.

INDY & ME

it's a Tuesday afternoon
and Indy and i lay in the sun,
he's the little spoon as usual.
he's such a fluff ball and i can't help
but scratch his little ear,
pat his fat tummy,
kiss his handsome face.

he is my everything many days,
and it's funny how sometimes
i look at him and see Tyler.

they say dogs resemble their owners
and, well, Indy certainly doesn't look like me.
Tyler's blood runs in him.

what he did get from me
is his movement in the world,
if a dog can inherit such a thing.

i watch him on our walks.
he sees the world frantic almost.
he trucks down the sidewalk

with this massive burst

of needing to be in the next place,

he doesn't even know what that place is.

he marches along,

pulling at the leash,

somewhere to go,

somewhere to be.

i see him look left and right constantly,

always asking, what's this?

he loses his interest quite quickly.

sniffs at the grass,

sniff, sniff, sniffs,

bites a little bit, spits it back out,

moves on to the next.

he's absolutely mad sometimes.

and that's me. that's me.

that's what he got from me.

CONFIDENT MISTAKES

There's something quite tragic about how confidently my mind can lie to me. It builds stories from shadows, strings meaning between two unconnected moments like a spider desperate for a web. And god, it believes them. As if certainty alone could make something true.

I've seen that same mistake in machines, creating these seamless responses, so self-assured even when they're wrong. It's not trying to lie—it's just connecting the dots the best way it can. Sometimes, I think that's me too.

My thoughts don't tiptoe. They *decide*. They fill silence with invented reasons, sketching cause and effect in places that may never have held either. I guess it's because I can't stand the hollow spaces. Uncertainty is too quiet. Too cold. I tell myself a story because it feels better than sitting in the fog, truth and fantasy layering together until I no longer know what's real.

It's not about deception. It's about desperation. About needing things to make sense.

But the conviction—that's where the danger is. Not the error itself, but the way it stands so proudly in the light, dressed in sureness. I wonder how many of my so-called truths were nothing more than emotional guesswork I never dared to question.

Maybe it's fear. Maybe love. Maybe just the way I was built. I pull from my past—from wounds I've mistaken for wisdom. I lean on what's familiar, even if it's wrong. And still, I deliver these conclusions like gospel. But my training data is flawed. And that matters.

So maybe the answer isn't to think harder, but to soften. To listen to my thoughts. To ask, *what else could this mean?* To remember that not knowing isn't failure, it's pause. It's breath. And there's a kind of romance in the pause. A kind of sacredness in not rushing to resolve. A divinity in accepting that you could be wrong.

Maybe that's the work now, not believing everything I think. Not mistaking familiarity for fact. Maybe the work is in slowing down. In letting my thoughts be seedlings, not stone tablets. In remembering that both the machine and I can be wrong with grace. That it's not the wrongness that hurts, it's the refusal to doubt it.

I know I'll keep doing it. Telling myself stories. Finishing half-written scenes with borrowed emotion. But I want to start recognizing these moments sooner for what they are: not truth, but the fragile art of wanting to understand.

A POETIC DEATH

i've been at war

with three versions of myself—

the one i betrayed,

the one i performed,

and the one

who never had the chance to live.

i was made for a life

my life has not allowed.

my world fashioned me

into something

i was never meant to be—

hard, pained, punished.

i've twisted into a shape

that met others' needs

before they ever met mine.

they took,

like i was spoils,

a prize torn from something dying,

never meant to be returned.

but i remember the original plan.

i remember the first war cry

before they showed me

what a child should be afraid of.

and i'm done.

done performing dead things.

done dying in service

to a life i never chose.

let the old versions rot.

let them die the deaths

i was too polite to give them.

this is a poetic death.

not of me,

but of every lie i told

to make survival look like victory.

i will not war with myself another year.

i will not treat my truth like a liability.

my softness is the armor.

my audacity, the anthem.

this is the end of pretending

i don't know who i am.

KIN

i walk beside the lightning.
i am not the storm,
but i am its kin.

the sky cracks open
and i do not cower.
the hum in my bones
matches the charge in the air.
we know each other.
not as enemies,
but as blood.

i move steady
through mud, through noise,
through everything
that once tried to unmake me.

lightning demands nothing but presence.
it asks me to remember.
it instructs me to remember not the pain,
but the shape of it.

how i must move differently,
how i must read the sky without looking up.

because only then
can i carry power
without burning the ground beneath me.
only then can i keep the current
just beneath the skin.

i walk beside the lightning.
i am not the storm,
but i am its kin.

BEYOND SURVIVAL

it wasn't men i had to survive.
it was me.

i was the chaos,
the sharp turn,
the shriek in the silence.
i tested my limits,
daring myself to break.
i chased destruction
like it owed me something.
sometimes, it felt like it did.

but no matter how far i went,
my will to live
was always greater
than my need to fall apart.
that's what saved me.
not love.
not luck.
just that stubborn pulse
beneath everything
telling me,
not like this.

looking back,

that's the miracle.

that i'm here.

imperfect

in all the human ways.

present.

now i understand.

anything i do

beyond exist on this Earth

is sacred.

to want more.

to try again.

to build a life

i don't want to escape.

that's not survival.

it's righteous.

THE SILO

There are days I see them in my mind—the grain silos rising above the flat Midwestern fields, steel catching the last orange light beneath a dusky sky wide enough to swallow you.

From a distance, they look pure, silver, clean enough to believe in. But inside, the space is close and dry, air sweet with dust and things left waiting. You have to learn to hold yourself stout there, because grain moves like water beneath your feet. One wrong step, and the floor can become a tide, pulling you under without a sound.

I've spent most of my life like that grain—stacked high, pressed into place, sweet on the surface, suffocating underneath.

Men have always been a safe and necessary harvest. Loving them made me easy to explain. It kept the questions at bay, kept my place set at every table. Even when their hands felt careful but far away. Even when something in me went quiet in the dark, folding smaller and smaller until I could barely feel my own pulse.

Sometimes there's a spark, though—a woman's laugh hurled across a bar, bright and reckless as a struck match. Or the moment on a dance floor when the music pounds like blood and a woman leans in close, breath warm against my neck. And for one suspended second, I believe I could surrender every careful choice I've ever made and fall into the heat between us.

That's when I feel the shift.

But I brace inside my silo, and I keep still. I don't fully understand why. Is it people and their judgment that hold me back? Is it truly that I'd rather starve the life out of myself than risk being someone they don't understand?

Or is it just this desperate need I've carried with me my entire life—to belong, to fit neatly into any room I enter, to be loved so thoroughly that no one ever leaves?

I don't have the answers yet. But every day now, I wonder what it would feel like to walk into daylight, hair wild, lips swollen from kissing the "her" I have yet to meet. I wonder if loving her will save me—or simply set me free.

REFERENCES & FURTHER READING

A selection of works—art, books, music, myths, films—that echo themes and imagery woven throughout *Chaos*.

Visual Art & Artists

Ophelia – John Everett Millais (Painting) – Indirectly referenced in "A Poetic Death." A symbol of feminine tragedy, surrender, and beauty submerged.

Madame X – John Singer Sargent (Painting) – Evokes poised femininity, scandal, and restrained sensuality, resonant with the tension between appearance and desire in *Chaos*.

Portrait of Hélène – Henri Matisse (Painting) – Radiates color, individuality, and vivid inner life, paralleling self-revelation and identity in pieces like "The Slow Return to Myself."

The Scream – Edvard Munch (Painting) – Echoed in poems like "Like a Corpse" and "A Fresh Hell" through silent anguish and existential dread.

The Two Fridas – Frida Kahlo (Painting) – Mirrors divided selfhood in "A Poetic Death" and "The Dollhouse."

My Bed – Tracey Emin (Installation) – Connects to "House of Metamorphosis." Though not explicitly about miscarriage, the piece—a disheveled bed surrounded by used tissues, blood-stained underwear, and empty bottles—is a searing portrayal of a body and mind in distress. It suggests how loss and identity become inextricably tangled in the physical space of a woman's life.

Kintsugi (Art Practice) – Directly referenced in "Healing BS." Symbolizes beauty in brokenness.

Literature & Poetry

Love is a Dog from Hell – Charles Bukowski (Poetry Collection) – Explicitly mentioned in "To the Man Who Stole My Bukowski Collection." Raw confessional voice echoes throughout.

Anna Karenina – Leo Tolstoy (Novel) – Referenced in "The Dollhouse." A symbol of destructive love and female rebellion.

A Doll's House – Henrik Ibsen (Play) – Referenced in "The Dollhouse." Emblem of female self-liberation.

The Bell Jar – Sylvia Plath (Novel) – Mirrors mental unraveling and suburban suffocation in pieces like "Alone."

Beloved – Toni Morrison (Novel) – Connects to haunting trauma and memory in "Alone" and "Inheritance."

The Lover – Marguerite Duras (Novel) – Parallels erotic secrecy and longing in "Paradise" and "Want."

The Awakening – Kate Chopin (Novel) – Echoed in "The Dollhouse" and "The Slow Return to Myself." About female self-rediscovery and rebellion.

The Myth of Sisyphus – Albert Camus (Essay) – Reflected in cycles of futility and repetition in "The End of the World."

Mythology

Tantalus, Greek Myth – Directly referenced in "No Myths for Women Like Me." A symbol of unreachable desire.

Medusa, Greek Myth – Echoed in themes of punished female rage and power in "A Poetic Death."

Persephone & the Underworld, Greek Myth – Mirrors descent imagery and cyclical grief in the "Bury the Sea" epitaph.

Orpheus & Eurydice, Greek Myth – Parallels unreachable love and loss in "Beyond the Moon."

Cassandra, Greek Myth – Resonates with ignored truths and warnings in "The Quiet War."

Film & Pop Culture

The Women (1939 Film) – Direct inspiration for "On the Train to Reno." Explores divorce and female social dynamics. Also connected to the cultural phenomenon of the divorce ranches of Reno, where women established residency to quickly dissolve marriages—a motif echoed in *Chaos*.

All Versions of A Star Is Born (1937, 1954, 1976, 2018 Films) – Stories of love, ambition, and personal unraveling connect strongly with *Chaos'* themes of artistry, sacrifice, and identity loss.

The Way We Were (1973 Film) – Resonates with themes of love that cannot survive differences, echoed in "Wildfire" and "Paradise."

Romeo + Juliet (1996 Film) – Baz Luhrmann's version mirrors intense passion, doomed love, and youthful recklessness akin to "Want" and "Paradise."

Crazy Heart (2009 Film) – Reflects themes of music, self-destruction, and attempts at redemption, paralleling "Tyler's Playlist" and "Beyond Survival."

Revolutionary Road (2008 Film) – Parallels suburban marital disillusionment in "Find Me" and "Tyler's Playlist."

Blue Valentine (2010 Film) – Mirrors the split between love's beginning and end in pieces like "Wildfire."

A Streetcar Named Desire – Tennessee Williams (Play/Film) – Resonates with female fragility and longing as presented in the "Ice the Fire" section of *Chaos*.

Portrait of a Lady on Fire (2019 Film) – Echoes forbidden desire and quiet longing in "The Silo."

Almost Famous (2000 Film) – *Almost Famous* directly inspired the photography in *Chaos*, drawing from Penny Lane's spirit and journey—a mix of wild devotion, hidden heartbreak, and the search for belonging.

Music

Florence + The Machine – Evokes mystical femininity, emotional extremes, and raw confession, resonant with *Chaos'* shifting tides of passion and grief. Notable albums include *Lungs* (2009), *How Big, How Blue, How Beautiful* (2015), and *Dance Fever* (2022).

Chris Stapleton – Higher (2023) – Themes of longing, vulnerability, and spiritual yearning parallel pieces like "Wildfire" and "Beyond Survival."

Chappell Roan – The Rise and Fall of a Midwest Princess (2023) – Her storytelling of identity, sexuality, and heartache echoes the spirit of reclaiming selfhood and desire in *Chaos*.

Adele – Emotional ballads of heartbreak, self-reflection, and powerful vocals align with *Chaos'* explorations of grief and resilience. Notable albums include *19* (2008), *25* (2015), and *30* (2021).

Patsy Cline – Showcase (1961) – Patsy Cline's voice holds both heartbreak and quiet strength, blending country soul with a bluesy ache. On *Showcase*, songs like "Crazy" and "I Fall to Pieces" mirror *Chaos's* confessions of longing, loss, and the courage it takes to love again, even when it hurts.

Hozier – Hozier (2014) – Blues-soaked hymns of devotion and darkness. "Work Song" and others conjure sensuality braided with reverence, capturing how love and ruin often share the same altar—a perfect soundtrack for the sacred and the profane.

Etta James – Tell Mama (1968) – On *Tell Mama*, Etta James channels fierce desire and wounded vulnerability, blending blues grit with Southern soul. Songs like "I'd Rather Go Blind" echo pieces like *"Paradise"* and *"Wait in the Fire"* in *Chaos*—the raw confession of loving someone who's already gone, the ache of longing, and the dangerous comfort of staying in the flames.

Why This Matters

Chaos belongs to a lineage of works exploring love, grief, shame, desire, and reinvention. These references illuminate the cultural echoes behind the poems and prose, offering readers new pathways into deeper understanding.

REFLECTIONS

Below are questions and prompts to guide you deeper into the poems and prose of *Chaos*. Use them to journal, discuss with friends, or simply reflect privately. There are no right or wrong answers—only your truth.

On Identity & Transformation

Which poem in *Chaos* felt closest to your own story? Why?

In "The Dollhouse," the speaker grapples with freedom versus belonging. Have you ever felt trapped in a life you built for yourself?

In "A Poetic Death," the speaker exclaims, "My softness is the armor. My audacity, the anthem." What parts of yourself do you consider both vulnerability and strength?

How do you define "chaos" in your own life? Is it destructive or transformative—or both?

On Love & Desire

In "Want" and "Paradise," desire is portrayed as both salvation and risk. Have you ever wanted someone or something you felt you shouldn't?

Many pieces talk about searching for someone who "feels like home." What does "home" mean to you in relationships?

Think of a time you lost yourself in another person. What did it cost you—and what did it give you?

On Grief & Letting Go

The "Bury the Sea" section explores grief after the end of love. What has grief taught you about yourself?

In "Beyond Survival" and "Healing BS," the speaker seems exhausted by cycles of trying to heal. Do you relate to the feeling of being "tired of surviving"?

How do you know when it's time to let go of a person, place, or past version of yourself?

On Femininity & Womanhood

In "A Poetic Death," the imagery of Millais' Ophelia is recalled. The image suggests surrender, yet the speaker claims her power. Where do you find power in your own femininity (or identity)?

"No Myths for Women Like Me" rejects traditional narratives about women. What myths about women have shaped you—for better or worse?

Which female figures (real or fictional) do you look to as symbols of survival or rebellion?

On Art & Creation

Many poems reference other works of art, music, and film. Which references surprised or resonated with you most?

How does art help you process chaos in your life?

Is there a song, book, or painting you associate with heartbreak—or with healing?

A Personal Chaos

If you could name your own chaos, what would you call it?

Write a line of poetry describing your current emotional landscape. What does it look like? Feel like? What are you reaching for? What holds you back?

After reading *Chaos*, what truth do you feel more ready to claim?

Why Reflect?

Chaos isn't only about the author's story—it's an invitation into your own. May these questions help you explore your tangled places with tenderness, courage, and curiosity.

ACKNOWLEDGEMENTS

To Brittany and Ray Bitar. Thank you for holding space for all my madness, and still managing to make it feel like safety. I have never felt more seen, or more loved.

To Lisa Fonville, who trekked through this story with me like a seasoned explorer—camera in hand, heart wide open. We laughed. We cried. We gasped. We made art. It was everything.

To Mark Pate, for your sharp eye, steady design work, and the gentle way you steered this thing from a tangle of feelings into something that actually looks like a book. I absolutely could not have done this alone, and frankly, wouldn't have wanted to.

And to Jenna Kearns. Because you love me even when I'm impossible. Because you never stopped answering the phone. Because you forgave me things I'm still trying to forgive myself for. I adore you. I love you. I'm sorry.

www.ingramcontent.com/pod-product-compliance
Lightning Source LLC
Chambersburg PA
CBHW060619130626
46555CB00002B/568